Get Happy with Dowsing

Change Unhealthy Patterns

Susan Collins

Get Happy with Dowsing
Change Unhealthy Patterns
Susan Collins

Kindle and Amazon Print on Demand Edition May, 2022
ISBN: 978-1-7781307-1-7
Based on the Print Edition: May, 2011
ISBN: 978-0-9780899-9-3
All published by: Susan Joan Collins
335 Patricia Drive, King City, Ontario, L7B 1H4, Canada

Check the other Kindle books by Susan Collins in the Complete Guide to Dowsing series on Amazon.

Print books by Susan Collins from www.dowser.ca
Bridge Matter and Spirit with Dowsing
Dowsing for Feng Shui and Space Clearing
Meet Alien Energy with Dowsing
Meet Orbs with Dowsing
Water Wells: What a Dowser Needs to Know
Life Cards Oracle System

Rent Dowsing Workshops from Susan's Vimeo page
https://vimeo.com/susancollinsdowser/vod_pages

Contact Susan susan@dowser.ca   www.dowser.ca

Praise for Susan's Work

"The depth and thoroughness of the investigations you have done in your protocols is a HUGE gift to students. The teaching is so clear and orderly and well-prepared it makes the material easily comprehensible. And you are very caring about your students. It's a true privilege to take your workshops."   Betsy, New Jersey, USA

"Thank you for a very informative course yesterday. You covered a vast amount of material in the three hours - It was most helpful and I shall go through the various worksheets again over the next few days to check that I really understand it all."   Liz, UK

"I love your perspective you are so real and genuine and no nonsense! I love spiritual work that is practical and applicable. The course was exactly the confidence boost I needed to continue practicing and now I know exactly what direction to take."   Stephanie, California, USA

"This context is EXACTLY what I've been looking for. I can tell that you love teaching, it's inspiring. I feel like I've struck gold, thank you very much!   Vanessa, Alberta, Canada

Table of Contents

1. **Introduction**

You can use dowsing, a natural biofeedback system, to transform your physical, mental, emotional and spiritual energies to create the life you want for yourself. This book will help you manage your energies to bring balance, harmony and happiness to all aspects of your life. You will eliminate barriers to your happiness, then create the energies that bring you the experience of happiness.

Dowsing can sometimes help balance quite dramatic difficulties and issues. It does this by connecting the conscious and subconscious minds with the body so that you can dig deeply into the underlying causes of unhappiness in a way that is both non-invasive and non-confrontational. It is convenient because you don't have to go to a clinic or hospital where an authority figure will be in charge of your process. You can learn to dowse for yourself in the privacy of your home, so it's free and readily available.

Once you've identified your issues and brought them to consciousness, you can use other dowsing techniques presented in this book to balance them and to activate your goals.

What is Happiness?

The definition of "to be happy" used to mean that someone was lucky, but the Welsh used the word to mean that someone was "wise". The difference in meaning is huge: it's the difference between thinking that happiness is something that is beyond our control and knowing that happiness is available to anyone with the wisdom to recognize it.

What creates happiness, and how can you stay happy? Do you have happiness that you acquire, or do you become happy because of your subjective perception of external conditions? It seems there are different ways to get happy depending on your perceptions.

What is happiness for you? Is it the "butterflies" you feel in your stomach when you're excited? The feeling of being in love and knowing you are loved? Is it the adrenalin rush you get from riding a roller coaster or mastering a video game? Is happiness the anticipation you feel when something pleasant is about to happen? Is happiness the satisfaction of good food and good company, or praise from your friends, family or co-workers? Is happiness looking at yourself in the mirror and liking what you see?

Happiness can come from the feelings of satisfaction you get after completing a task such as cleaning the house or after a trip to the gym or from helping someone. It can be the feeling of relief that you have enough food in the house to feed your family, or that your child made it home safely in the dark. Happiness can be many things. Profound happiness can be found in the freedom to be and express who you are with another human being without judgment.

This kind of happiness can sometimes be felt in our relationships with animals. Pets don't judge us or hold grudges no matter who we are or what we do, and they don't care what we look like or how much money we have. A pet can feel like a true friend and bring happiness even though they may not feel emotions exactly the same way we do.

What would make you happy right now?

Is your happiness based on waiting for someone to do something for you? Like getting a present on your birthday or winning the lottery? Does happiness seem like an external force, and if you could just read the right book or find the Happiness Store, you'd be fine? Or does your heart tell you that happiness is something that is generated internally, that it's simply a process of choosing to live well? If it was as simple as just choosing to be happy, then wouldn't we all just choose it?

Sometimes we know things with our hearts and minds but can't act on them. Dowsing can assist you in activating happiness in your life.

Being happy can make us jump for joy!

Clearly happiness is subjective. We're human, and the human experience is filled with pain and challenges. The experience of physical pain is quickly forgotten. For example, women can remember that childbirth hurt, but they don't continue to feel the physical pain of it after the body heals. Emotional pain lasts much longer – the heartache of loosing someone we love through rejection, illness, or circumstances can last a lifetime and prevent us from moving on to form new relationships.

If you're in pain, can you be happy?

When we remember painful events, our brains take us right back to the time and place where the event happened, and some people never move on, living in a desperate, solitary state that feels like a personal hell. How do we change that?

We tend to live in the world of "If Only". *"If only I had more money ... if only I could find someone who understood me ... if only I had paid my bills on time."* It does no good to live in the If Only world. Happiness is experienced in the present moment. Most of us, barring disaster, usually have enough to eat and a place to live, but not many people can say that they are happy all the time.

One reason is that we tend not to notice when we're happy. It's often the lack of happiness that triggers self-examination. Most of us focus on what's wrong instead of what's right. Focussing on problems tends to reinforce them.

Haven't we read enough books yet?

Don't we know enough to be happy already? The answer is a qualified "YES". Our minds are full of the advice we've read and heard, but it's often hard to translate that mental knowledge into the heart where we can both create and experience that state of emotional well-being that we call happiness.

In this book we will connect the head and heart with dowsing (an ancient biofeedback technique of detecting and transforming energy) to help you change unhealthy patterns in your life and create the conditions within yourself that will produce the experience of happiness. Along the way you may find that your life-force energies increase.

What is life force energy?

We humans are made of many parts: physical, mental, emotional, spiritual and energetic. We have spent our lives learning about the first four aspects but not on our energy self. For many of us, our energy systems are an undiscovered country: our modern lives haven't prepared us to manage our life-force energies. Some cultures call life-force energy chi or prana, and some societies teach their children how to work with their energy through meditation or other practices. In the West, we generally haven't yet incorporated the knowledge and management of life-force energy into the general fabric of our lives.

What do I, Susan, know about being happy?

I know that happiness is something you have to work at, and the path to happiness is often through some sort of emotional or physical crisis.

When I was 29 I became geriatric. I was diagnosed with Rheumatoid Arthritis and had trouble walking and using my hands. Western medicine didn't really help much, though the drugs I took over the next twenty some years enabled me to lead a "normal" life and raise two children. I was not happy about my physical state, although other aspects of my life were in balance.

My search for physical health brought me to dowsing and through dowsing techniques I learned to balance my physical, emotional, mental and spiritual energies and as of this writing, I haven't been on prescription medications for almost two decades and I generally enjoy good health.

Life is a process, of course, so my search for personal happiness is an ongoing quest.

This book began (and continues) as a workshop that I've been teaching for several years. People who have attended workshop sessions say that this material has helped them change destructive patterns in their lives and has helped them to experience happiness.

Every time I work with this material personally, I am reminded of non-beneficial behaviours I need to change. Life is a process, and we are never perfect, but it is very satisfying to see that we can all make beneficial changes in our lives. And that makes me happy.

2. How to Get Happy

This book teaches you to use dowsing to help you get happy. First, we will provide the basic instruction on how to dowse accurately. You can use the methods presented here to first identify your personal barriers to happiness, and then to create new, healthy thought patterns and neural pathways.

(Those who are interested in learning more about dowsing can refer to my website www.dowser.ca or my other books on the topic, listed at the end of this book.)

How are thought patterns created?

What you think about all the time creates linkages in your brain. The more you think about certain things, the stronger these neural pathways become. If you are constantly thinking about the problems in your life, then your brain "map" will be composed mainly of problems. Dowsing can be an effective way to help you consciously and unconsciously divert your attention away from the things that make you unhappy, and towards the things, people, events and circumstances that will bring you happiness.

The first step is to set your Intention to create the results you want in your life. This book will guide you through a process to create healthy thought patterns and neural networks which will result in the experience of increased happiness. The book can help you avoid difficult circumstances as well as consciously create health in all aspects of your being so that you can get on with what you're meant to be doing!

For best results, read this book in sequence.

Each section of the book builds on the previous one. Read and make notes as suggested, starting at the beginning. If you follow the steps and do the work in the order laid out, you will get better results.

If you have trouble doing the work in steps, consider that this might be one of your issues (write it down!) Simply choose to read the book front to back, following suggestions along the way. Sometimes you may have to go back and repeat a step to resolve multiple issues, but if you skip any steps, your results may be disappointing. It takes time to review the material, but it will be worth it!

This book is designed to help you create happiness in your life by guiding you to:
- Dowse with accuracy.
- Find unhealthy conscious and unconscious patterns.
- Identify healthy goals and patterns.
- Disconnect unhealthy patterns.
- Activate healthy patterns.

This is your transformative work, and it will work powerfully if you intend what is best and appropriate not just for you but for everyone! For example, if someone in your life is "making" you unhappy with their constant complaining, then one way of improving the situation is for you to create a bio-field around you to act as a buffer. This will help you sustain your own energy in the face of life's daily challenges. You may know people who never seem to lose their life-force energy, no matter what is going on around them. You can create that state for yourself using the techniques presented here.

Basic Dowsing Information

The basic information of how to dowse is presented here with everything you need to know to get started. More advanced dowsing information is given in my other books. (See back.)

If you don't already know how to dowse with a pendulum, check out Appendix 1 for instructions.

The Dowsing Protocol is given in full in Appendix 2. Have a look at it. At first you will probably need to read the text while running your pendulum for confirmation of the steps. Over time, you will commit the Protocol to memory. The more you use it, the easier it gets and the better your results will be. In an emergency you can "trigger" the Protocol with a word, phrase or action, but do it in full AT LEAST once a day for best results.

A brief Glossary is given at the end of the book so that you are familiar with basic dowsing terms.

The more you help others, the more you help yourself. There is more than one path to reach your goal. Simply beginning something has its own power.

What are the keys to success? They include the ability to focus your mind, the will to help your Self and the courage to begin.

You Will Need:

- A notebook to use as a journal as you work through the material.

- Water to drink. Dowsing works best if you're well hydrated.

- A pendulum. Anything that swings freely will do: a necklace, a key on a string, or have some fun shopping for a "real" pendulum.

- Your issues and goals! Don't worry if you don't know what they are. This book will give you some exercises to identify them. Make headings in your notebook and write down whatever issues and goals come to mind now.

3. The Dowsing Tools

The primary dowsing tools are you, a pendulum (see Appendix 1 for instructions on dowsing with pendulums if you don't already know how to use one.) and the Dowsing Protocol (Appendix 2). I also make extensive use of the PLUS/MINUS Chart (below). Before you begin a session, you should be rested and, in a calm, relaxed state. If you dowse when you're upset, your results won't be very accurate. Learning to use the tools is easy. Learning to relax and focus your mind at the same time takes practice.

Changing long-standing unhealthy patterns will probably take more than one session. Don't be discouraged if you have to repeat the process a few times. Just as with gradual weight loss, even the best diet takes a committed effort over time to be successful.

Dowsing Protocol

When you begin as a dowser you might wonder if you're just fooling yourself when the pendulum moves one way or another. You may not trust your answers. The Dowsing Protocol helps you be both accurate and safe while you dowse. It will help you develop your intuition so that you can trust the answers you get with dowsing.

Use the Dowsing Protocol every time you dowse. This practice will help you to access the energies that are affecting you and your state of happiness. If you don't use the Protocol or some other sort of energy management and protection system before you dowse, it would be like picking up the phone, dialling random numbers, and taking advice from whoever answered. If you start with the Protocol before you dowse, you'll get your answers from the "Divine Source" (or however you address your highest spiritual principle), and the answers will be more accurate. With the Protocol you will never be given more energy or information than you can handle.

The Dowsing Protocol I'm sharing with you in Appendix 2 may seem like a lot of trouble to go through, but if you use it before each session, your accuracy will increase. You may also find that you experience more happiness and balance in your life as you "clean up" the energies around you. Feel free to adapt the Protocol to your own traditions.

I recommend doing the Protocol in the morning and before you go to bed at night in addition to before each dowsing session. I believe doing so will help all aspects of your life. You can also "trigger" the full Protocol with a word or phrase if you really need to dowse and don't have time for the full Protocol. I trigger the Protocol every time I take a sip of water, so I am generally well-prepared for any emergency!

The full Dowsing Protocol is given in Appendix 2. If you send me an email at susan@dowser.ca, I will send it to you as a free, two-page Pdf.

Dowsing Protocol Summary

1. Balance your physical body.
2. Connect to your dowsing consciousness.
3. Forgive yourself.

4. DISCONNECT nonbeneficial energies.
5. MAXIMIZE beneficial energies.
6. Seek permission to dowse.
7. Dowse.
8. Create an Energy Matrix if needed (automatic energy system).
9. Disconnect.
10. Thank.
11. Communicate your results appropriately.

People often ask for specific wording for different situations. The Protocol I'm providing is a template that you can adapt to every situation by substituting a few words. When you go through it the first time at the start of a session, your intention is to prepare yourself for accurate dowsing (Steps 1 – 6).

In Step 6, focus on the specific issue you are addressing. For example, you could dowse for permission (from the Divine Source) to dowse for your underlying subconscious patterns that are creating unhappy situations in your life, or you could focus on something else in your life such as which food choice would best support your health at this time. Adapt Step 6 to your needs.

Allow the pendulum to swing freely as you go through the Protocol and ask it to indicate YES to show you that the steps are complete. If you get a NO response at any stage, you know you need to resolve, as best you can, that step before going on. For stubborn issues, use "Create an energy Matrix" (Step 8) to reduce nonbeneficial barriers and increase beneficial influences over time.

(For a more detailed explanation of the Dowsing Protocol and the use of other tools, please refer to my Kindle / Amazon book Dowsing That Works or my other print books, available from www.dowser.ca.

The PLUS / MINUS Chart

Once you've figured out how to get YES and NO answers with a pendulum (Appendix 1) and are familiar with the Dowsing Protocol (Appendix 2) you may be wondering how to tell the difference between a really big YES (something that is very true for you) and a little YES (something is true, but not really so important). And it's important to understand the degree of NO your pendulum is indicating. The amplitude and speed of the pendulum swing will be an indicator, but an even better way to tell the difference is by using the PLUS/MINUS Chart, below.

To begin using the chart, start with your pendulum swinging over the centre line that points to zero. Next, focus on your question, and ask the pendulum to swing to the number and line that best reflects the degree to which the question is true for you. For example, the overall benefit of eating white sugar for most people would be MINUS 10, the overall benefit of drinking pure water would be PLUS 10.

If you don't have a physical chart handy, use your hand. Spread your fingers wide. Your index finger can be zero, the left fingers can represent the MINUS scale, and the fingers on the right of the index finger can represent the PLUS scale. I also often use the edge of a table as a baseline, and just imagine the chart is there. The reading can be just as accurate as having a paper chart in front of you.

At the beginning of each dowsing session, after you have done the Dowsing Protocol, use the PLUS/MINUS Chart to check your accuracy. Ask your pendulum to swing to the line and number that best represents how accurate your dowsing is at this time. If it is less than at least PLUS 8, use the Dowsing Protocol to DISCONNECT all nonbeneficial energies that are interfering with your ability to dowse accurately. Then use Step 5 to MAXIMIZE your accuracy. Check your accuracy again and get it to as high a reading as you can before you begin.

Sometimes your accuracy can slip if your subconscious mind feels that your conscious mind won't like the true answer. You'll know your accuracy is slipping if you get unusual answers. I always ask for "The Truth" as appropriate. I say "as appropriate" because I don't want to be given more than I can handle or information that isn't my business and doesn't relate to the issue I'm

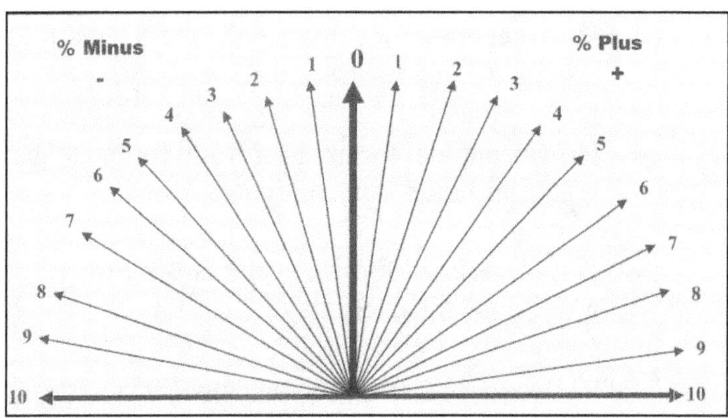

Readings on the left side of the chart are MINUS (NO or nonbeneficial). Readings on the right side are PLUS, (YES or beneficial).

working on. Asking for the truth and for change to occur at the appropriate rate will keep things moving easily within your comfort range.

Your level of accuracy can also drop off if you are tired, hungry, thirsty, intoxicated or sick. If your physical state is in low energy, you may have to try again when you're feeling better. You can also go back to the Dowsing Protocol and repeat the steps to see if you can bring your accuracy up to a reasonable level. If you are chronically fatigued all the time, just do the best you can. Your health will gradually improve.

Practice with some simple questions such as:
- How beneficial for my health is it for me to drink about a quart (litre) of water a day?

- How beneficial for my health is it for me to drink more than a quart (litre) of water a day?

- How beneficial for my health is it for me to drink less than a quart (litre) of water a day?

- How beneficial for my health is it for me to get less than four hours sleep a night?

- How beneficial for my health is it for me to go for a walk outside every day?

Come up with your own practice questions.

Once you are comfortable with simple practice questions, gradually introduce questions that don't have obvious answers such as the ones that follow. The power of dowsing is that you can discover information that is uniquely true to you at a particular moment.

Dowse the following questions:
- *"Pendulum swing to the number and line on the PLUS / MINUS Chart that best represents what my energy level should be."* (For me the pendulum swings to PLUS 10. Your optimal energy level may be different or fluctuate.) Make a note of your optimal level.
- *"Show me my energy level when I am happy"*
- *"Show me what my current energy level is now."*
- *"Show me my average energy level over the past week."*
- *"Show me my average energy level when I am around _________ (person's name)"*
- *"Show me my energy level when I eat chocolate"* (or name another substance that you suspect weakens you)
- *"Show me my energy level when I think about __".*

Think of other examples of circumstances that "make you" feel weak or strong and check their effect on your energy level using the PLUS / MINUS chart.

Keep track of your readings. The list of examples can go on, but hopefully you're getting the idea that you can use dowsing to see what effect different thoughts, experiences and emotions can have on your overall vitality and happiness.

Blind Dowsing

It can be hard to dowse for yourself and the people you love, especially about emotional issues. You'll get the answer you expect unless you are detached from the outcome because your emotions may cloud your accuracy. You'll have the best results if you dowse from a place of ignorance and apathy: you don't know the answer and you don't care what it is. Another way to say that, is that dowsing works best from a place of detached compassion. You see the problem, but you stand apart from the problem.

If you can detach from the problem, relax and stay calm you'll be better able to access your intuitive ability, and to reprogram your life.

One way to detach from the dowsing outcome is to "blind" dowse. Here's how you do it: first write the various options or answers on identical cards (or put them in identical white envelopes) and shuffle them face down on a table. Then dowse which card or envelope best represents the correct answer to your question at this time. Doing this will get your thoughts and emotions out of the process because you won't know which answer is on which a card which and so can't consciously influence the pendulum to move in the way that you want or expect it to.

If you blind dowse, always include a card which says "Other" in case none of the options you've written down has accurate information for you.

Think of an issue in your life. Write down different courses of action you're considering on separate pieces of paper and put them in identical envelopes. Don't forget to include an "Other" envelope. Mix up the envelopes and see which one has the best information for you at this time. Use the PLUS / MINUS Chart to fine tune how appropriate the answer is for you at this time.

Practice!

4. The Emotional Body

Emotions can interfere with our ability to dowse accurately.

Emotions can be constructive or destructive depending on the circumstances. Sometimes anger can give us the energy to take action when it's needed, but if we stay angry our body systems remain over-stimulated and our health suffers. Sometimes love works against us and we are afraid to lose what we love, so we become virtual doormats for another person.

Should we pretend we don't feel bad sometimes? No. On the other hand people don't want to hear us complain all the time, so sometimes we suck it up and shut down the parts of our heart that feels. It is healthier to acknowledge one's emotions than to try and suppress them. It's good to resolve issues in a timely way rather than ignoring them and hoping they will go away. Strong emotions tend to explode eventually.

Of all our different body systems, our Emotional Bodies may be the hardest to think clearly about because the intensity of our feelings clouds our judgment. We may be upset by something and not really know why. We may fool ourselves into thinking everything is fine because we are afraid of the future if we admit our pain. Inside many of us is a crying child that has never felt understood or loved. We may feel alone, or unwanted or unattractive and may take elaborate steps to find comfort. I've painted a grim picture of our emotional workings and while most people don't stay in the dark places very long, it's easy to find ourselves there occasionally. I invite you to consult a health professional to discuss potential treatments for prolonged destructive mental and emotional conditions.

Emotions around issues

Not all emotions are bad of course. Without love we wouldn't be here as a species. We love and love creates love, and the world works together. Emotions are only a problem if they interfere with our ability to make good choices.

It's hard to think clearly when our emotions are running hot! Whether the emotions come from abuse or from ecstatic love, the effects can be the same: we make bad decisions. The expression "love is blind" refers to this state. We must be extra careful when making life and health choices when we are very emotional. We may not have a clear idea of the accuracy of our perceptions when we are blinded by love. Very strong emotions can trigger the survival responses of the Sympathetic Nervous System and the "fight or flight response". Appendix 3 details signs of emotional abuse.

Balance your emotions

The primary thing to do in any nonbeneficial circumstance is to stay in control of your emotions and thoughts so that you can think clearly enough to gather accurate information to make good decisions to take appropriate actions that result in successful ongoing outcomes. Don't panic! Take whatever measures are necessary to make sure you are safe. As much as possible, control your reactions to what is going on around you. Being able to think and feel clearly will help you bring yourself to your full power and maintain your health and happiness. Even if you don't believe you are strong enough, act as if you are, and you will become stronger.

Situations are often resolved by taking action. If you can release fear and judgment, you will be able to remain in control of your Emotional Body. How can you do that quickly when you feel your emotions rising? An efficient way is with Emotional Freedom Technique which we will review in the next section.

Please see Appendix 3 for information about emotional abuse.

Emotional Freedom Technique (EFT / Tapping)

In addition to using dowsing to remove nonbeneficial emotions, I often recommend clients do Emotional Freedom Technique (also know as EFT or "Tapping") to cope with destructive emotions and even Post-Traumatic Stress Disorder (PTSD). EFT was developed by Gary Craig and his website (www.emofree.com) offers many excellent, free resources for self care.

EFT works by encouraging the body systems not to shut down when confronted by an emotional memory by self-tapping different parts of the body and repeating simple statements.

EFT Simplified Version

Here is a simplified version of the full EFT protocol. I like it because I don't have to remember where all the tapping points are all over my body. I also prefer the karate chop shown in the photo to the gentle tapping of the fingers, because if I'm upset it feels good to pound the sides of my hands together while saying the statements.

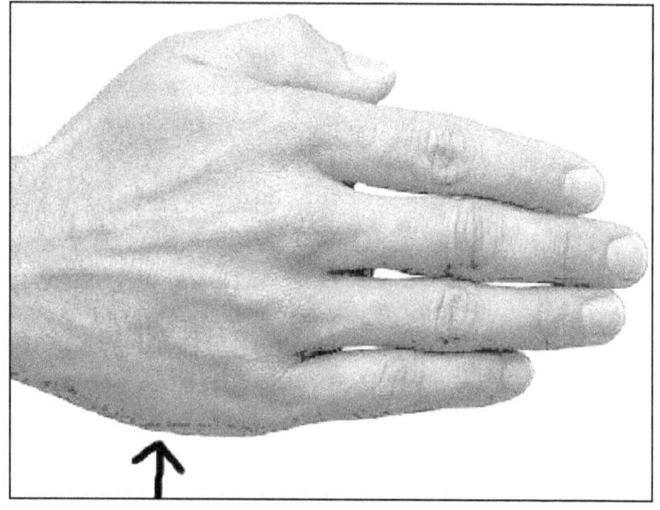

The "Karate Chop" point

1. Do the Dowsing Protocol.

2. Think of an issue in your life. How much does it bother you on a scale of 1 to 10? (Use the PLUS / MINUS Chart)

3. Do the "Karate Chop" (energetically tap the sides of your hands together) while saying the phrase three times: "*Even though I* (name the thing bothering you) *I deeply and completely accept myself*". (See sample statements below.)

4. NOW how much does it bother you on a scale of 1 to 10? Repeat until the issue no longer bothers you or is reduced. Stubborn issues may take some time to

resolve. Try different wording to get at stubborn pockets of resistance.)

Sample EFT statements:

"Even though I (get upset with my partner) I deeply love and completely accept myself"

"Even though I (often get sick) I deeply love and accept myself."

"Even though I (eat too much candy) I deeply love and accept myself."

"Even though I (sometimes feel like nobody likes me) I deeply love and respect myself."

"Even though (it seems like things are out to get me) I deeply love and respect myself."

"Even though (there are many things I am afraid of) I deeply love and accept myself."

Using EFT helps us be aware of a situation without being crippled by it. The path of the Spiritual Warrior is to do one's best and not be attached to the outcome. Being in a detached state increases dowsing accuracy.

Ho'oponopono Practice

Four statements from the Ho'oponopono Hawaiian tradition that can help resolve emotional conflicts are: *"I'm sorry. Please forgive me. Thank you. I love you."* These simple statements, expressed in a way that is comfortable for you, can help move a discussion forward if there are problems in a personal relationship. Perhaps the statements are not made all in the same conversation, but the idea is to acknowledge past hurts and harms while reinforcing positive relations.

Not only is it important for you to make these statements to resolve conflicts, but it can also be important for the other person to be able to communicate them. It may take the other person some time to be able to respond, because of this way of communicating is not what we do every day. Even if the other person isn't able to respond, you can do your part. (These are statements and questions I dowse through at end-of-life situations and when doing Spirit Release.)

Following is the essence of the Ho'oponopono exchange. Adapt it to your own words and timing.
- *"I'm sorry.   Are you sorry?*
- *Please forgive me. I forgive you.*
- *Thank you.   Do you thank me?*
- *I love you.   Do you love me?"*

Check Your Belief Systems

Sometimes our belief systems hold us back. Dowsing can help us to understand what our subconscious mind truly believes and to transform nonbeneficial patterns.

Get your pendulum in motion, then read the following statements out loud. If you get a YES when you read a statement, then it is true for you at this time. If you get a NO, it's an indication that this is an area where you need to do some work. Try to gracefully accept these answers without self-recrimination as they are clues to your underlying issues.

Dowsing sometimes feels like playing a game of "Twenty Questions" with the Universe. In the game, you ask a series of questions to try to figure out what the other person is thinking about. In this case, your subconscious is the "other person", and dowsing can allow the subconscious to express itself in a way that your conscious mind has trouble doing.

Dowse the following statements. Remember to record any NO responses you got in these belief statements so you can go back and transform them later.

1. I am worthy of happiness.

2. I deserve to be happy.

3. I want to be happy.

4. I am able to be happy.

5. I am responsible for my own happiness.

6. I am able to make choices that bring me happiness.

7. I am worthy of respect, love and money.

8. I am able to share my happiness with others.

9. I trust myself.

10. I love myself.

Add your own belief statements that you think reflect your conscious core beliefs and dowse if your subconscious mind believes them.

Any belief statement, above, that resulted in a NO answer is an item you can adjust with the Dowsing Protocol. Make sure these items are recorded in your journal.

We've reviewed the importance of the Dowsing Protocol and how to work with your emotions and belief systems. Before we move on to using dowsing to transform nonbeneficial patterns, let's review some of the traditional ways of creating happiness.

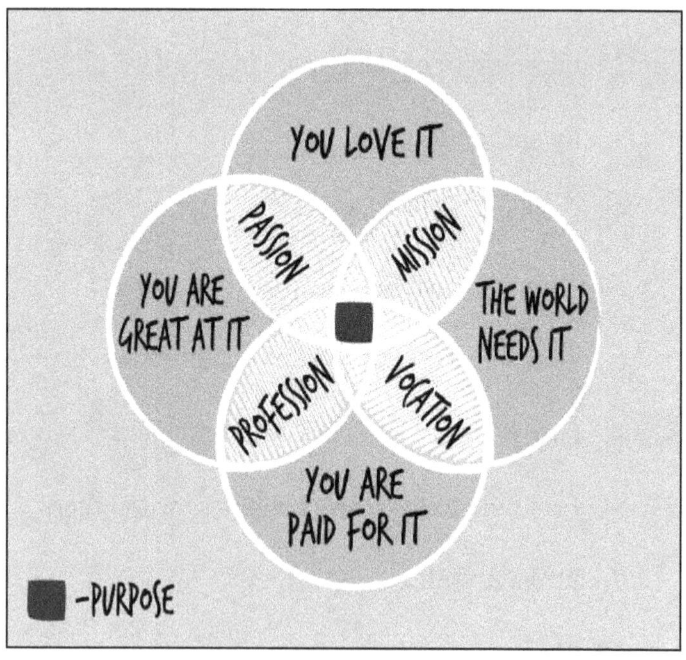

Here's another way of thinking about choosing goals.

5. Plan to Change Patterns

Before we change unhealthy patterns with dowsing, I'd like to review some of the traditional methods of changing behaviours, so that you have a complete transformational tool kit with which to work.

This book is meant to be read in sequence. You should be making notes as you go along. There is no race to finish reading the book (or living your life) to discover a secret at the end. The secret is to commit now to start the process of transformation.

Make a S.M.A.R.T. plan.

Make your plan to transform your life and create happiness SPECIFIC, MEASURABLE, ACHIEVABLE, RECORDED and Time SPECIFIC.

What are your SPECIFIC Goals?

Write your answers to each question below in your journal. Jot down the first things that come into your mind, no matter how silly or how seemingly impossible. You can come back later and add whatever you like.

I would like to be ...
> Examples: I would like to be happy. I would like to be in a good job with lots of money. I would like to be better friends with my children. I would like to be healthy. I would like to be good looking. What else?

Dowse:
How beneficial would it be for me if I was that? (Use the PLUS / MINUS Chart)
Am I willing to be that?
Am I able to /be that if I dowse and take action?

I would like to feel …
Examples: I would like to feel beautiful. I would like to feel loved. I would like to feel healthy. I would like to feel successful. I would like to feel that my life matters. What else?
Dowse:
How beneficial would it be for me if I felt that? (Use the PLUS / MINUS Chart)
Am I willing to feel that?
Am I able to feel that if I dowse and take action?

I would like to know …
Examples: I would like to know enough to get a good job. I would like to know how to make friends. I would like to know how to lose weight and keep it off. I would like to know how to cook a meal that people enjoy. What else?
Dowse:
How beneficial would it be for me if I knew that? (Use the PLUS / MINUS Chart)
Am I willing to know that?
Am I able to know that if I dowse and take action?

I would like to have …
Examples: I would like to have lots of money. I would like to have a family that gets along better. I would like to have the respect of my friends. I would like to have time to myself. What else?

Dowse:

How beneficial would it be for me if I had that? (Use the PLUS / MINUS Chart)

Am I willing to have that?

Am I able to have that if I dowse and take action?

I would like to do …

Examples: I would like to do the best I can all the time. I would like to visit Europe. I would like to go dancing/golfing/to the movies/read books whenever I want to. I would like to do the things I want to do instead of what everyone else wants to do. What else?

Dowse:

How beneficial would it be for me if I did that? (Use the PLUS / MINUS Chart)

Am I willing to do that?

Am I able to do that if I dowse and take action?

How will you MEASURE Your Success?

Make a note of the steps you expect to take as you progress towards achieving your goals.

Is your plan ACHIEVABLE?

Set realistic steps. For example, if you want to get fit, your first goal would not be to run a marathon. Reach your goal by planning the steps it takes to get there. To get fit, your first step might be to walk around the block, then to walk quickly around the block, then to run, then to run further and so on. Try to create happiness step by step by recognizing the milestones you need to reach to create the overall experience

How will you RECORD your plan?

Record your successes and failures. Why did you win? Why did you slip? How can you adjust your plan for future success?

What is your TIMELINE?

What is the timeframe in which you expect to reach the steps of your goals? Say, for example, *"I choose to stop smoking this Friday night at 8 pm"* instead of *"Someday I'm going to stop smoking"*. Prioritize your actions. When you wake up in the morning, decide what is the most important thing you will try to accomplish that day.
  Dowse:
    How realistic is my timeline? (Use the PLUS / MINUS Chart)
    Am I willing to meet that timeline?
    Am I able to meet that timeline if I dowse and take action?

Learn from Past Experiences

If you want to change bad eating habits, and you know that when you go grocery shopping you always pick up candy when you go down the snack-food aisle, then next time you shop, don't go down that aisle! Pick up something you've never tried before that looks like it's healthy and read the label to see if it's a healthy choice. Of course, you can just dowse to see if it's a healthy choice but reading labels for nutrition and additives is a good habit to get into.

Don't beat yourself up when you slip. Since we're human, we know we're going to make mistakes once in a while. Take a breath and start each day again. Stay calm. Be flexible. Even if you fail once or multiple times, it doesn't mean you've failed. Acknowledge your limitations and give yourself another chance.

As the band Chumbawamba, in their song Tubthumping, sang, *"I get knocked down, but I get up again. You are never gonna keep me down."*

Don't Let Other People's Fear Stop You

In long marriages and other relationships, changes will occur in the relationship over time. Give each other permission to be the people you are now, not the people that you were ten, fifteen or fifty years ago. Perhaps one partner wants to change the job they've always done. This can create fear in the other partner, thinking that the income, or hours or loss of personal time may threaten their family life.

Sometimes we get locked into other people's expectations of who we are. For example, perhaps you've always cooked dinner, and you think it's time that other people started doing more around the house. Letting people know your feelings and setting up a transition plan is a good way to start. Encouraging others to help develop a plan can be a good way to get them enthusiastic about contributing more. So what if your teenager makes pizza every time it's their turn to cook?

Find support

Take responsibility for yourself but ask for and accept help when it is offered. You may prefer to keep your goals secret to nurture your dreams before letting other people know about them. In this case, people may not offer to help. On the other hand, if you let people know what your goals are, they may help you achieve them. Decide which approach works best for you.

Maintain a sense of humour

Some days you'll just have to laugh at yourself and your circumstances and set your sights on doing better tomorrow. You may change your goals over time and that can be a healthy evolution. Don't feel guilty about taking a break. Just don't forget to come to your plan and dowsing.

Barriers to Goals

It can be hard to know where the barriers are to achieving our happiness goals. Here is a list of sources to dowse. Dowse each for YES and NO responses, then use the PLUS / MINUS Chart to check their degree of influence. (Remember to journal your answers!).

Try looking at things in a new way
to see a different perspective.

6. Conscious and Unconscious Patterns

As we review the times we've succeeded or fallen short of our goals we can sometimes see pattens emerge. We can point at external reasons such as our personal family history, or the place we grew up in, or limited finances, or abuse suffered, or any number of things to credit or blame for the way things have turned out so far.

What will drive success is our determination to choose to take actions today to create the future we want. Let's look at conscious and unconscious patterns that may be limiting your happiness.

Sometimes we kid ourselves about what we want and what we're willing to do to get it. Most people say they want to be a healthy weight, but fewer people are willing to diet and exercise. For many, the short-term pleasure of indulgent eating outweighs the future reward of a healthy body. Most people say they want to be in loving relationship, but not everyone is willing to work through the inevitable difficult times. (That being said, no-one should stay in an abusive relationship. If this is your situation, seek professional counselling. Appendix 3 discusses emotional abuse.)

Sometimes we unconsciously sabotage ourselves because we are afraid of failing. For example, some children slack off at school and accept bad marks because they think that if they don't try, they never really fail.

The next section will help you see if your conscious desires about what you want in your life correspond to your subconscious beliefs. Both your subconscious and conscious belief systems must be in alignment for you to experience true happiness. If they are not in alignment, you may be in a state of cognitive dissonance which will make it very difficult to reach your goals.

Simply making statements while dowsing is a way to do a reality check. Whatever statement generates a NO is an area where nonbeneficial energies need to be DISCONNECTED (Step 4 of the Protocol) and beneficial energies need to be MAXIMIZED (Step 5 of the Protocol). Remember that to make ongoing energy adjustments you use Step 8 of the Protocol.

Conscious Patterns

A conscious pattern is any habitual behavior where you realize you have a choice and do the unhealthy thing anyway. People make more resolutions to start something than they do to break a bad habit. But we know from Step 4 of the Dowsing Protocol (Appendix 2) that we have to DISCONNECT nonbeneficial energies so that there is space to form new patterns MAXIMIZING happiness (Step 5).

Think of washing a floor. As we progress, we need to empty the bucket of dirty water and replace it with clean water. Steps 4 and 5 of the Protocol will guide you to first DISCONNECT nonbeneficial energy, then to MAXIMIZE beneficial energy. Step 8 will guide you to create an Energy Matrix, an ongoing, automatic system to maintain good energy so that you can achieve your goals.

Examples of conscious patterns

You may already have some examples of conscious patterns in your journal, but here are other examples of areas where nonbeneficial conscious patterns express themselves. Dowse to see if any are true for you.

- **Exercise**: you buy the membership, but don't go.

- **Work habits**: you mean to do some work but end up watching TV or playing computer games.

- **Eating habits**: you want to eat healthy food but can't resist sugary snacks.

- **Addictions**: you want to stop smoking, drinking, or using drugs, but can't do it.

- **Relationships**: you try not to argue, but you just can't help yourself.

Jot down the patterns you want to modify today.

It can be useful to figure out the underlying source of a pattern, but it is not always necessary to do so. Dowse to see if it is necessary to find the originating source or if you can proceed directly to transforming all known and unknown nonbeneficial patterns to create ongoing happiness in your life.

If it is beneficial to you to explore why you have a pattern, don't wallow in the past with it. If your dowsing directs you to clear out the energies that no longer serve you, then do so without spending too much time examining your history, unless your dowsing specifically directs you to do so.

For example, maybe you're afraid to speak up for yourself now because when you were a child your older siblings (or parent or teacher or someone in a store) made fun of you when you tried to express yourself. Dowse if this is true for you. If you find this is true, remind yourself that you are grown up now, and that it doesn't matter today what happened fifteen or fifty years ago. It's your choices and actions today that will determine the rest of your life.

What Creates Conscious Patterns?

Remembering an event where you tried and were unsuccessful can create an unhealthy conscious pattern. We can all go back in our lives and remember times when things didn't work out as we had planned. The memory of these events can alter our brain structures by creating islands of memories. Over time, these islands can form larger masses by developing new neural pathways between them. These continents of nonbeneficial memory can eventually become the dominant feature of our brains and personalities and hold us back from even trying to achieve our goals.

What fires together wires together in our brains. In other words, you get what you think about. You can rewire your brain creating new, beneficial neural pathways by reinforcing beneficial affirmations with dowsing. The old neural pathways dissolve if energy does not flow through them, so don't dwell on the bad old days.

Dowsing affirmations is a good way to create new, healthy neural pathways. Part of your brain will eventually start believing what you repeat to yourself. If you have trouble believing a supportive affirmation (such as *"I am worthy of respect, love and money"*), you can act as if the statement is true by saying something like "*I will act as if I am worthy of respect, love and money*")". Pretend you are even if you don't always feel that way. Ask yourself how you would act if you were confident in yourself, then act that way. Acting as if something is true can help it become true.

Why do Unhealthy Patterns Persist?

Unhealthy patterns persist because there may be a greater reward for continuing the pattern than there is for resolving the pattern. For example, when someone is ill, friends and relatives may treat them kindlier than they normally would. Friends might bring them food and look after them and give them lots of attention. With so much positive reinforcement of their illness, where is the patient's motivation to get better? Some people, unconsciously, choose to stay ill because the reward for doing so is greater than the discomfort of their illness.

What's the pay off for keeping unhealthy patterns? Sometimes you get money, shelter, love, glory, prestige to stay in a situation that is unhealthy.

What's the trade off for keeping unhealthy patterns? Even though you may have shelter and money, you may suffer from physical, mental and emotional stresses created by your inner conflicts.

What's the payoff for creating healthy patterns? When we are living our lives based on healthy principles and are living in resonance with our authentic selves, discomfort can fall away, and we may have the opportunity to experience lasting happiness.

Conscious barriers to achieving my goal are

Fill in the blanks at the end of the following statements, then dowse to see how true they are for you.
- My emotional state (I get so upset when …)
- My belief system (I know I can never …)
- My habits (I wish I could stop …)
- Because …

Journal down the patterns you are willing to modify today.

Affirmations to Rewire your Brain for Happiness

For each of the following affirmations you want your pendulum to confirm the statement with a YES response. You can also use the PLUS / MINUS chart to confirm the degree to which these statements are true for you at this time.

If you get a NO to any statement, make a note of it and use Step 4 of the Protocol to DISCONNECT any nonbeneficial energies or processes associated with the statement and Step 5 to MAXIMIZE beneficial energies and processes that support the statements.

Do the Dowsing Protocol (Appendix 2). With your pendulum for confirmation, say out loud:

1. I am safe and protected when I dowse.

2. Dowsing helps me achieve my goals.

3. I am worthy of respect, love and money.

4. I am strong and healthy in all aspects of my being.

Consider going back and reviewing the affirmations on page 29.

Unconscious Patterns

Unconscious patterns can be formed by mental "triggers" a word, sight, sound, smell or taste that sets off a chain of memories that takes you back to a place or time where something happened that you don't remember now. Because of what happened then, you are programmed to respond in a specific way because of the consequences of what happened last time.

Unconscious patterns are triggered in the Amygdala part of the brain which holds emotionally traumatic memories that cannot be consciously remembered. The "Flight, Fight or Flee" response of the Sympathetic Nervous System is known as the Amygdala Hijack when it is triggered by non-threatening events. People who have been in extremely upsetting situations may be involuntarily brought back to their mental state during the crisis by a benign trigger event.

For example, if the trauma occurred in Spring and you could smell lilacs while it was happening, now the smell of lilacs may make you panic. Or perhaps smelling the cologne of a former partner can make you sad if you sit beside someone on the bus with the same scent. Or perhaps hearing a sudden loud noise makes you feel like you are under attack. These reactions are referred to as Post Traumatic Stress Disorder (PTSD).

Unconscious patterns can be responsible for: uncontrolled emotional responses when you're driving; unsuccessful dieting; relationship failures; negative self talk; not pursuing goals because of fear of failure and other "knee jerk" reactions.

Dowsing can be used to detect unconscious memories storied in the Amygdala. Once they are brought to consciousness, they may be more easily transformed using the Dowsing Protocol.

Sample Unconscious Patterns

Dowse to see if you have any of these patterns on average. How great an impact do they have on you? (Use the PLUS / MINUS Chart.)

Outdated survival mechanisms?

If in the "bad times" there wasn't enough to eat, now you eat extra, or hoard supplies because part of you never got over the time when you couldn't afford what you needed. You act is if the bad times will never end.

Outdated commitments?

If when you were growing up your parents said, *"Don't talk to strangers"*, now you can't easily form friendships because you're afraid to talk to people. Or if your loved one said they would never leave you, but they did leave, you may have trouble trusting anyone new.

Inherited blocks?

If you think, *"Well everyone in my family was an alcoholic, so I guess I'll be one too."* or, *"Everyone in my family got cancer at 46, so I guess I will to."* you may be creating those futures for yourself. Studies have shown that children who have been adopted into families where they all get breast cancer, get cancer at the same rate as their adoptive families, even though there is no genetic reason for it.

Parts of soul damaged?

When traumatic things happen, for example just before a car crash, assault or other traumatic event, a fear response may put part of the "soul" into hiding. I believe this is a natural self-protection mechanism that avoids the potential experience of pain at or near death. In my opinion we don't lose our soul parts, so we don't need to retrieve them. Our soul parts may be damaged and hiding in the body, perhaps creating addictions. If we can repair the soul parts, we may be able to eliminate addictions and restore full human functionality.

Dowsing can help heal and reintegrate damaged soul parts. A statement to initiate soul repair is to address all the parts of our Selves that are missing and say: *"It's OK to come back now. I survived. I'm all grown up and I'll take care of you."* Ask for your soul parts to be reintegrated at the appropriate rate. Use the Dowsing Protocol to guide the process.

Negative self talk?

The words we use to describe ourselves can also create nonbeneficial unconscious patterns. If you call your child a brat as a nickname, they may grow up fulfilling that vision.

Letting go of words, memories, thoughts and ideas that no longer serve you is an important step towards happiness. Don't think of yourself as a "victim of abuse". You are a "survivor of your life experiences".

Archetypes and Roles

Psychologist Carl Jung brought the idea of archetypes to western medicine in the last century. "Archetype" is a word that describes a pattern of behavior or energy. For example, someone who embodies a WARRIOR archetype will feel inclined to fight for what they believe is right. Someone with a KING archetype will want to make the rules for everyone, and someone who carries a SLAVE archetype will allow themselves to be bossed around.

Just because someone carries the energy of a particular archetype, it doesn't mean that they had a past life as someone in that role. For example, some people, when they're exploring past life "experiences" remember themselves as being Cleopatra or Abraham or some other historical figure. We can't all have been Cleopatra, but many of us may carry the energy archetypes (behaviour patterns) that the role of an ancient QUEEN may have exhibited.

Sometimes knowing that we carry an archetypical behaviour may help us in this life. For example, if we know we carry the energy of a TEACHER in this life, it can help us find a career path that will make us happy.

On the other hand, if we discover we carry the energy of a SLAVE in this life, it is probably something we want to get rid of. The following exercise will help you identify some archetypes that may be active in your energy field. Make notes as you go through the lists so that you can balance these archetypes later.

Archetypes (Roles) and Vows Exercises

Find out what roles and vows are active in your field on average. Check to see if they are beneficial or nonbeneficial to you. If they are nonbeneficial, you can use the Dowsing Protocol to reduce or DISCONNECT them. If they are beneficial, you can MAXIMIZE them as appropriate for greater happiness.

Do the Dowsing Protocol (Appendix 2). Use a pendulum to dowse a simple YES or NO answers.

If you find a certain role is active in your field on average, use the PLUS / MINUS Chart and dowse: *"To what extent is that role beneficial to me on average?"*

Current Archetypes and Roles

Dowse for each archetype from the list below: *"Is the energy of being a _________ active in my energy field on average?"*

Artist / Bodhisattva* / Child / Creator / Entertainer / Explorer / Healer / Helper / Hermit / Hero / Holy Person / Judge / Lover / Magician / Maiden / Martyr / Outlaw / Parent / Rebel / Royalty / Scrooge / Seeker / Servant / Slave / Student / Teacher / Trickster / Victim / Warrior / Wisdom Keeper / Other** / None

* A Bodhisattva is someone who has made a vow to remain in the world until all sentient beings are enlightened. (Buddhist tradition.)

** If dowsing shows you OTHER as an answer, think of other roles not listed that may apply.

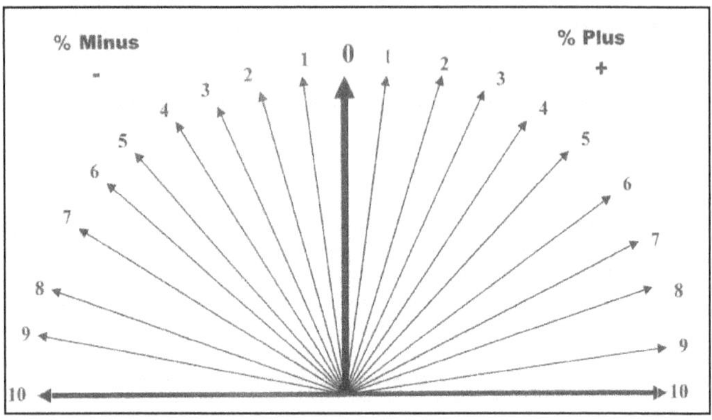

Optimal Archetypes and Roles

Dowse for each archetype from the list below, *"What energy archetypes or role would help create happiness in me now?"*

Artist / Bodhisattva / Child / Creator / Entertainer / Explorer / Healer / Helper / Hermit / Hero / Holy Person / Judge / Lover / Magician / Maiden / Martyr / Outlaw / Parent / Rebel / Royalty / Scrooge / Seeker / Servant / Slave / Student / Teacher / Trickster / Victim / Warrior / Wisdom Keeper / Other / None

Use the PLUS/MINUS chart and dowse, *"To what extent would creating that archetype's energy in me assist me in experiencing happiness?"*

Current Vows

Find out what vows are active in your field on average. Check to see if they are beneficial or nonbeneficial to you. If they are nonbeneficial, you can use the Dowsing Protocol to reduce or DISSCONNECT them. If they are beneficial, you can MAXIMIZE them as appropriate for greater happiness.

Do the Dowsing Protocol (Appendix 2). Use a pendulum to dowse YES or NO answers.

Dowse for each vow from the list below: *"Is the energy of the vow of _________ active in my energy field on average?"*

Abstinence / Allegiance / Celibacy / Citizenship / Fidelity / Guilt / Invisibility / Obedience / Legal / Masonic / Medical / Marriage / Military / Penance / Personal / Poverty / Professional / Religious / Renunciation / Seclusion / Service / Silence / Truthfulness / Other* / None

If you find a certain VOW is active in your field on average, use the PLUS / MINUS Chart and dowse: "To what extent is that vow beneficial to me on average?"

Optimal Vows

Dowse for each vow from the list below, *"What vows would help create happiness in me now?"*

Abstinence / Allegiance / Celibacy / Citizenship / Fidelity / Guilt / Invisibility / Obedience / Legal / Masonic / Medical / Marriage / Military / Penance / Personal / Poverty / Professional / Religious / Renunciation / Seclusion / Service / Silence / Truthfulness / Other / None

Use the PLUS/MINUS chart to dowse: "To what extent would creating that vow's energy in me assist me in experiencing happiness?"

Having completed the exercises above you should now have a list of archetypes and vows that are currently active in your energy field and their level of influence on you. You also have a list of optimal archetypes and vows that would assist you in experiencing happiness and reaching the goals you identified in the previous sections.

Before you use dowsing to DISCONNECT the energies you've identified that no longer serve you and to MAXIMIZE the energies that will assist you in experiencing happiness, check again to see if any of your belief systems are preventing you from reaching your goals.

Vows can persist through lifetimes and prevent the natural evolution of the Soul.

7. Transform Unhealthy Patterns

In order to create new healthy patterns which will lead to happiness, you will first get rid of the old self-limiting patterns. It's a bit like emptying dirty water out of a bucket before you add clean fresh water. Energy flows like water and you've probably read about the old Zen master who keeps pouring tea into the young student's cup, even after it is over-flowing. When the student questions his teacher, the master replies: *"How can you learn anything when you are already full up."* If you are full up with old, nonbeneficial issues and patterns, then it will be hard to find space for health and happiness.

Are there other patterns to transform now?

Review your notes, then check to see if there are any other patterns that you need to, or are appropriate to, transform now. Review the lists you've made of things and energies in your life that you are ready to get rid of and to see if it is complete for now.

You can come back later and add more nonbeneficial conscious and unconscious issues, archetypes, vows and patterns as you think of them. You can also dowse a statement that says: *"I ask to DISCONNECT all known and unknown nonbeneficial patterns and transform them to beneficial, as appropriate for me at this time and on an ongoing basis."*

Your list of things to change probably has several items on it. How do you know where to begin? With dowsing, of course! Timing can be critical for resolving an issue and there may be a certain order you need to follow for best results. Sometimes people like to start with their major issue first or start with their minor issue first. Do this work when you are comfortable and have time.

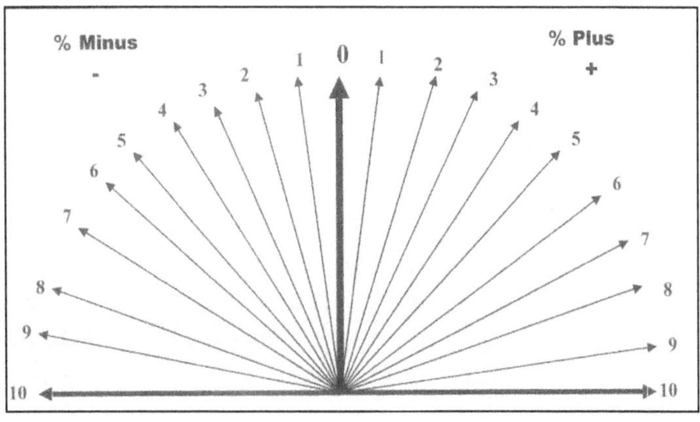

Dowse which patterns to transform first.

Slide your finger down the list of patterns you have identified and ask your pendulum to swing clockwise at the pattern you should transform first.

If you know from the previous exercises that you have issues about getting a good job, swing your pendulum back and forth over the 0 position on the PLUS/MINUS chart and ask, *"Show me the overall effect on me of worrying about getting a good job"*. The pendulum might swing to the MINUS 8 position on the chart, so that you know this worry is very bad for you and is reducing your vitality. On the other hand, if the pendulum swings to MINUS 2 on the chart, it would indicate that the worry on this issue is not so great, and that perhaps you should focus first on the other issues you've noted

If you don't know exactly what to work on, you can make a statement something like: *"I ask to transform all patterns that no longer serve me so that I am in balance and experience happiness."* Life would be lovely if we could transform all our issues with one statement in one session. It can happen that quickly, but I find the best results come from isolating the issues and working on them in detail.

With practice this whole process becomes easier. The use of a general statement such as the one above is more appropriate as a daily energy touch up. Just as we need to bathe regularly to remove daily sweat and grime, we need to refresh our energies regularly with simple exercises such as the ones given here.

DISCONNECT patterns

The next step is to DISCONNECT unhealthy patterns. Later you will activate the healthy energies and patterns that will allow you to experience happiness in all aspects of your life.

Refer back to the primary issue or pattern you decided to transform first.

1. Do the Dowsing Protocol

2. Think of the pattern you want to DISCONNECT while measuring your energy with the PLUS / MINUS Chart.

3. DISCONNECT the pattern. (Step 4 of the Dowsing Protocol). With dowsing tool in hand say: *"For the best and highest good and as appropriate, I ask that all nonbeneficial energies (emotions, thought forms,*

attachments etc.) and processes (biomechanical, biochemical, bioelectric) associated with every aspect of my being (physical, mental, spiritual, emotional and energetic) be immediately removed in all dimensions, time frames, realities and frequencies including all nonbeneficial energies that are known, unknown, hidden, secret, stealth, disguised, fluctuating, fractal, reversed, residual and potential including all nonbeneficial cellular memories and energy triggers, including all nonbeneficial psychic cords and quantum connections." (If the tool continues to DISCONNECT after repeating the above three times go to Step 8.)

The motion of the pendulum reflects the state of transformation. If it keeps moving, keep repeating and revising the statement you are making up to three times, perhaps changing some of the wording as it occurs to you. The tool will stop when the energy is disconnected. You may have to say personal things that aren't written in this book in order to disconnect the pattern or patterns you're working with.

Sometimes, but not always, people experience a sensation in their bodies during the DISCONNECT phase. It could be anything from a slight headache, nausea, weakening muscles, a tingly sensation, a brightening of the environment, or even tears. These sensations are normal and useful because you know "something" is happening. Don't be alarmed; complete the process.

When the DISCONNECT motion of the pendulum ends, ask: *"Is the pattern still active in my energy field?"* If YES, you may need to repeat the DISCONNECT at a later time. You can also set up an Energy Matrix, Step 8 of the Dowsing Protocol, to create gradual transformation.

If the pendulum indicates NO (the pattern is no longer in your energy field), ask if there are other patterns to disconnect at this time and continue the process.

Use your PLUS / MINUS chart to see the current impact of the pattern after the previous DISCONNECT cycle. Say: "Show me the overall effect of having this pattern in my life." Make a note of the number. Ask if you can reduce the impact any further at this time. If YES repeat DISCONNECT process above. If NO, proceed to Chapter 10 Activate Healthy Patterns.

Repeat until you bring the energy impact to neutral (0), or your dowsing says that the pattern is transformed as much as possible for this moment. The DISCSONNECT phase may take your energy reading to a PLUS number on the chart.

Once you have disconnected all the patterns that are appropriate for you to disconnect at this time, move on to the next chapter. You can come back and do more transformational work at another time. Let the dowsing guide you – don't try to force the process. Fundamental change can take some time to integrate, so always ask for results to be experienced at the appropriate rate.

Activate Healthy Patterns

Once you have DISCONNECTED unhealthy patterns, it is time to activate the healthy energies in your life that will bring you the experience of lasting happiness. Refer back to the notes you've made through the course of the book and review the Dowsing Protocol to make sure you're not taking shortcuts!

Set your intention to experience happiness in your physical, mental, emotional, spiritual and energetic beings, and in all aspects of your personal and professional relationships and endeavours. Don't settle for just getting to an 80% beneficial level, aim for 100% beneficial energies in all aspects of your life. (You may not get to 100% in everything, but it's a good goal!)

It may take longer, even a few years of personal work, to achieve lasting happiness, but the time goes by anyway, and you may as well be doing something useful! Please remember that since we're human, there will always be times when things don't seem perfect, and we aren't happy. Use the techniques presented here to restore your health and happiness when things start to degrade.

Activate your goals

1. Do the Dowsing Protocol.

2. Think of the goals and patterns you want activate (one at a time). *"I would like to be ... feel ... know ... have ... do ..."*

3. Maximize your energy field. With dowsing tool in hand ask: *"that my energy field be maximized for the best and highest good of all creation and as appropriate that all aspects of my physical, mental, spiritual, emotional being exist in perfect health in all dimensions, time frames, frequencies and realities and that I am guided in my thoughts, actions, and choices to be in resonance with the Divine Source."* (If the tool continues to

MAXIMIZE after repeating the above three times go to Step 8 Energy Matrix to continually create the conditions for happiness.)

Ask that an ever-changing Energy Matrix be established in the appropriate place, staffed by the appropriate beings, that will automatically adjust and transform all nonbeneficial energies and processes to beneficial as appropriate.

4. Ask if there are other patterns to transform at this time. If YES, check your notes and continue the process.

Energy Matrix Broadcasting

Energy broadcasting is a method of sending balancing energy at a distance using objects to help us focus the dowsing power of our hearts and minds.

Broadcasts can be set up with anything you have at hand. Instead of using a magnet as in the method described below, you could use some combination of crystals, candles, symbols, or whatever objects dowse as appropriate. Sound is often a powerful element in a broadcast.

1. Do the Dowsing Protocol
2. Determine the issues.
3. Install broadcast using:
   Base (clean cloth or paper)
   Witness (photograph, hair, signature, name, etc.)
           Objects - dowsed
           Affirmations - dowsed
   Magnet, crystal, copper (or other energy device)
4. Intend that the appropriate balancing take place.

5. Time how long the broadcast should operate.
6. When the time has elapsed, check to see if the broadcast is complete.
7. Dismantle when finished.

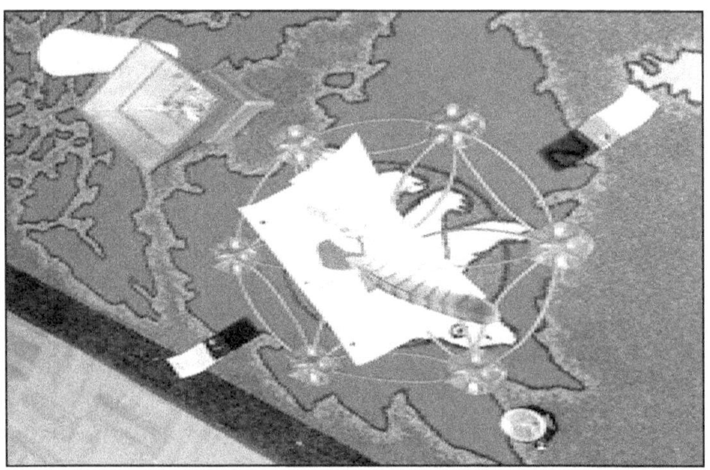

An energy broadcast. Seen here are written affirmations and dowsed objects placed to assist transformation.

Follow-up Suggestions

- Check and adjust your energies regularly with the PLUS / MINUS Chart. Dowse:

  - *"Is the old pattern still active in my energy field?"* If so, DISCONNECT it with Step 4 of the Protocol.

  - *"Is the new pattern active in my energy field?"* If not, activate and MAXIMIZE it with Step 5 of the Protocol.

- *"Please show me my current energy level."* If it is below PLUS 10, use the Dowsing Protocol to adjust it.

- *"Do my thoughts, actions, words and deeds support happiness?"* If not, adjust with the Protocol.

Barriers to success

We may experience barriers to success on our path to happiness. Dowse to see if any of the examples below apply to you:

- **You don't believe you are a good enough dowser to have success.** Even if you're not sure you're good enough to be successful, act as if you are. Use the techniques in this book and keep practicing. Sooner or later, it will work for you.

- **You don't feel worthy of doing this work.** We all have both the right and the responsibility to help ourselves, and others, as much as we can.

- **You feel too unhappy and emotional to do the work.** This is the place where you get to choose what the rest of your life will be like. Choose to do these exercises and practice as much as you can.

Even if you don't fully believe it's possible to change things in your life so that you can experience happiness, it's up to you to choose it, then act on it. Work on things bit by bit, keep practicing, and over time, you will achieve what you set out to do.

Change Unhealthy Patterns Summary

1. Do the Dowsing Protocol.

2. Measure your energy level with the PLUS/MINUS Chart.

3. Make a list of your goals

4. Make a list of your issues and unhealthy patterns.

5. Dowse with which issue to begin.

6. Do the Dowsing Protocol to DISCONNECT nonbeneficial patterns. Ask for change to occur at the appropriate rate.

7. Do the Dowsing Protocol to MAXIMIZE beneficial energies. Ask for change to occur at the appropriate rate.

8. Do the Dowsing Protocol to create an Energy Matrix (automatic system) that will bring your energies into perfect balance so that you can experience happiness.

9. Track your energy with the PLUS / MINUS Chart.

10. When complete, dowse to see if there is anything else to do to create happiness at this time.

11. Close the session.

8. Conclusion

Will dowsing magically make you happy and fix everything in your life? Probably not. We each need to work at being happy.

People tell me I'm lucky because of the way things turned out for me. I tell them I'm not lucky, I worked at it! Every day I do my best to stay conscious. I do my best to detect the dynamic physical and energetic forces around me and to figure out which of them support me and my goals. Dowsing is the most powerful tool I have ever found to help me do this.

My goals have changed over the years as the world has changed around me. None of us live in the world we grew up in. We each have unique life experiences. Some of them good, some of them not so much. Let's take what we've learned from the journey, and make a better, happier world for ourselves and for those around us.

Be in the moment. Resolve the past. Create your future.

Susan

Appendix 1
How to Dowse with Pendulums

Anything that moves can be a dowsing tool. The common tools are pendulums, L-rods, Y-rods, Bobbers and body sensations. The tools amplify our body's sensory perception; they are not being "controlled" by an outside force. Addressing the tools by the names "L-rod!", "Pendulum!") helps to focus the mind/body connection. Please see my other books for a thorough discussion of how to use tools. The pendulum and L-rod information presented here will serve you in most situations.

HOW TO USE PENDULUMS
Do the Dowsing Protocol
The basic movements of the pendulum are swinging back and forth, either away from you or across your body, or swinging in circles, either clockwise or counterclockwise. There are other subtle movements that you will begin to recognize as you develop a personal vocabulary.

The first step is determining what YOUR responses mean. Your responses may be different from another person's.

- Hold the string between your thumb and first finger, about 10 cm (3 inches) from the weight at the end. Use your dominant hand.

- While slowly swinging the pendulum back and forth, say out loud, "Pendulum, show me YES". The pendulum will move.

- If there is no response, swing the pendulum clockwise for a few seconds (if that is what you'd like your YES response to be), and say: "Pendulum this is my YES." Then repeat the question "Pendulum, show me my YES." Keep doing this until the pendulum moves on its own.

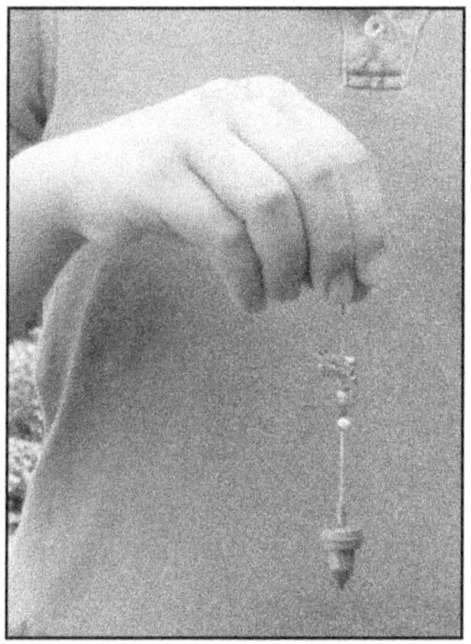

- Repeat these steps for a NO response, swinging the pendulum in the opposite direction.

- Repeat these steps for DISCONNECT and MAXIMIZE responses. The MAXIMIZE motion is often the same as the YES motion. The DISCONNECT motion is often the same as the NO motion.

- Find the motion for NEGATIVE electrical charge (often the same as your NO) and POSITIVE electrical charge (often the same as your YES response.)

- Find your POINT TO response using a chart for practice. (See section on Charts)

- Find NEUTRAL (often a diagonal swing)

- If you have different motions of the pendulum, first find your YES and NO, then find out what the other motions indicate by asking YES and NO questions.

- Test your responses with questions you already know the answers to.

Appendix 2
Susan Collins' Dowsing Protocol

ALWAYS use a dowsing protocol before you dowse to help make your answers more accurate and keep you safe. Hold the pendulum in your dominant hand while saying these words to confirm your answers. Use the first 5 steps of this Protocol to get YOURSELF ready to dowse. Then check with Step 6 to see if it is right for you to dowse on a particular topic at this time. If YES, then apply Steps 4, 5 and 8 to the issue to create lasting results. If NO, try again later, reword the question or try to work out why you are getting a NO response. When done, close the session (Step 9).

1. Balance your physical body (YES response)
Find a quiet time and focus your Intention to balance and ground every aspect of your being.

2. Connect to your Dowsing Consciousness (YES responses)
Say: *for the best and highest good* (or however you address the Divine) *I ask: to be connected to my human body for my good health, to be connected with the intelligence and beneficial energies of nature, to be connected and in resonance with Divine Good, to be connected, guided and protected by my Spirit Team and that that my dowsing be 100% accurate."*
a. Check the tool's signals for YES and NO
b. Check the tool's signals for DISCONNECT and MAXIMIZE

c. Set your INTENTION: what do you want to accomplish in the session?

d. Ask for the assistance of beneficial energies in resonance with you and the Divine Source who have useful information to share at this time to assist you in gathering information so you can make decisions and take appropriate actions to achieve your Intention as appropriate within your Territory. (Your Territory is the physical and energetic area you have a right to work within.)

e. If you are working with a client ask that these beneficial energies also be in resonance with them.

f. Check for the presence of the beneficial energies you asked for in d, above.

g. Confirm that they are aligned with the Best and Highest Good.

3. Forgive yourself (YES responses)

We cannot be accurate if we have not forgiven ourselves and those around us.

Say: "Creator, forgive me. I forgive myself. I forgive all those who have harmed me. I release them from my body mind and spirit. I ask all those who I have harmed to release me." If you cannot forgive someone, give them back the accountability for their actions. You are a survivor not a victim.

4. Clear yourself of non-beneficial energies
     (DISCONNECTING responses)

With dowsing tool in hand say: "For the best and highest good and as appropriate, I ask that all nonbeneficial energies (emotions, thought forms, attachments etc.) and processes (biomechanical, biochemical, bioelectric) associated with every aspect of my being (physical, mental, spiritual, emotional and energetic) be immediately removed in all dimensions, time frames, realities and frequencies including all nonbeneficial energies that are known, unknown, hidden, secret, stealth, disguised, fluctuating, fractal, reversed, residual and potential including all nonbeneficial cellular memories and energy triggers, including all nonbeneficial psychic cords and quantum connections. (If the tool continues to DISCONNECT after repeating the above three times go to Step 8.)

5. Maximize your energy field
(MAXIMIZING responses)

I ask that my energy field be maximized for the best and highest good of all creation and as appropriate

that all aspects of my physical, mental, spiritual, emotional being exist in perfect health in all dimensions, time frames, frequencies and realities and that I am guided in my thoughts, actions, and choices to be in resonance with the Divine Source. (If the tool continues to MAXIMIZE after repeating the above three times go to Step 8.)

6. Seek permission to dowse (YES responses)
If you get a NO to any of the following questions, do not proceed AT THIS TIME.

May I dowse for _______? (Permission)
Can I dowse for _______? (Ability)
Should I dowse for _____? (Is it for the best?)

7. Dowse.
- Use the processes described in Steps 4 and 5 above and apply them to the situation for which you are dowsing.
- Dowsing works best when you're in a state of ignorance and apathy: you don't know the answer, and you don't care what it is.
- Keep the question clear and literal.

- Assume nothing.
- Use a chart for accuracy.
- Respect others' privacy. Don't dowse unless requested to
- Dowse in service for others, not for personal greed.
- Never diagnose or offer medical, legal or financial advice unless you are a licensed practitioner.

8. Create a Matrix if needed (Energy System)

If the situation doesn't resolve itself within a few minutes, ask that an ever-changing energy matrix be established in the appropriate place, staffed by the appropriate beings, that will automatically adjust and transform all nonbeneficial energies and processes to beneficial as appropriate within your Territory.

9. Disconnect (DISCONNECTING responses)

Fully, consciously, actively and as appropriate at this time, disconnect from all energies with which you have been working. (You may stay connected to the Divine Source and your Spirit Team and other energies that need time to "cook" to integrate properly. Making sure you are disconnected from other nonbeneficial energies will ensure you don't stay in resonance with them which could create fatigue, disorientation and even illness.)

10. Thank

Thank all energies and Beings that have assisted you.

11. Communicate your results appropriately

If you are dowsing for someone else, be sure to check which results can be communicated to them for the best and highest good. Never discuss anything with anyone in a way that could identify the client. Be discreet.

Adapt this protocol to your needs by changing or adding any other words or prayers that feel right.

If you don't have time to go through it all, say something simple like: "Bless this situation." It's better to say a quick, simple prayer, even "BLESS YOU" at the moment it's needed than nothing at all because you don't have time to go through the whole protocol.

Please see Susan's books for more information on the Dowsing Protocol and other dowsing techniques, available from www.dowser.ca.

Appendix 3
Emotional Abuse

There is that story about a frog in a pot of cold water. The frog is comfortable and doesn't jump out. The water is heated gradually. The frog isn't as comfortable as it was, but still doesn't jump out. Eventually the water gets very hot and the frog is cooked!

Following is an inventory of emotional abuse symptoms, courtesy of www.healthline.com. Behaviours like the ones listed may come from an abuser's insecurities or mental health issues. Think of a situation or a relationship in your own life and review the listed behaviours. See if you recognize any of these circumstances. If you do, consider making an action plan. (See section 2.2)   that will help you regain a healthy environment. In the sections that follow we will look at constructive emotions that can assist your action plan. We will also review Emotional Freedom Technique to help you tame unproductive emotions.

Signs of Abuse

They:

- call you names
- say rude things about you
- have angry outbursts
- make patronizing remarks
- treat you like a child
- embarrass you in public
- dismiss your opinions
- make the decisions
- make foolish jokes about you
- are sarcastic towards you
- insult your appearance
- belittle your accomplishments
- put-down your interests
- provoke you
- make threats
- want to know where you are
- spy on you digitally
- control finances
- lecture you
- order you around
- feign helplessness
- are unpredictable
- walk out of discussions
- blame you for everything
- make you feel guilty
- deny they are abusing you
- accuse you of abuse
- demand respect
- won't communicate
- come between you and your friends and family
- withhold affection

- ignore you
- call you needy
- interrupt you
- dispute your feelings.

Not all of the behaviours listed above may be present in an abusive relationship, but if some are present, it may be a trend. Don't be like that poor frog in the pot as the water heats up!

Review the list above, do you recognize any of your own behaviours towards other people in your life?

If you are being abused, you may feel:
- unhappy in the relationship, but fear alternatives
- neglect your own needs for the sake of theirs
- ditch friends and sideline your family to please the other person
- frequently seek out the other person's approval
- critique yourself through your abuser's eyes, ignoring your own instincts
- you make sacrifices to please the other person, but it's not reciprocated
- you would rather live in the current state of turmoil than be alone
- bite your tongue and repress your feelings to keep the peace
- feel responsible and take the blame for something they did
- defend your abuser when others point out what's happening
- try to "rescue" them from themselves
- feel guilty when you stand up for yourself
- think you deserve this treatment

- believe that nobody else could ever want to be with you
- your abuser says, "I can't live without you," so you stay

What to do if you are being abused

If you fear immediate physical violence call 911 or your local emergency services. If you are not in immediate danger but want to find out what your options are, get in touch with counselling and legal services in your community. Find them on the internet or call a government office.

Meanwhile:

1. Decide that you won't respond to abuse or get sucked into arguments.
2. Disengage from the abuser and set personal boundaries.
3. Protect your children.
4. Limit exposure to the abuser as much as possible.
5. Ask for support from groups, friends and family members.
6. Make an action plan to keep yourself safe and healthy.
7. Don't give up.
8. Give yourself time to heal.

You can also increase emotional health with the Dowsing Protocol. You can disconnect nonbeneficial emotions and situations and create beneficial ones on an ongoing basis. Please review the Dowsing Fundamentals information in the Appendices for how to dowse safely and accurately.

Appendix 4: Brief Dowsing Glossary

Ancestors: the energy of the relatives of the current or former occupants or owners of the home or land.

Being: a conscious intelligence existing in the physical and/or other dimensions. Nonbeneficial beings are sometimes called "Entities".

Bodhisattva: In the Buddhist tradition someone who has made a vow to remain incarnated until all sentient beings are enlightened.

Brain Waves: Electrical activity in the brain. Trained dowsers can access all brain wave states simultaneously.

Ceremony: actions to create a result.

Chakras: energy centers in the body. The Nervous System.

Clairsentient: the ability to know things in other dimensions.

Cognitive Dissonance: mental discomfort from holding conflicting beliefs.

Conscious Mind: the aware, knowing, awake mind.

Deja Vue: the experience of having experienced an experience before.

Divine Source: a personal highest spiritual principle or consciousness. God.

Dimension: as of this writing, there are eleven known dimensions. "Normal" senses only give us access to four (Three-dimensional space plus time).

Dowsing: A biofeedback practice.

Dowsing Consciousness: the part of your Self that can access information from the quantum field.

Dowsing Protocol: a method to safely access your natural intuition.

Electromagnetic: having both electric and magnetic character and being positively or negatively charged.

Energy Field: region of electric, gravitational, magnetic or other subtle energy influence.

Entity: a nonbeneficial, other-dimensional being.

Energy Vampire: a being that feeds off someone else's energy.

Extra Consciousness: an awareness attached to a person which is not part of the individual.

Feng Shui: Chinese art of Geomancy.

Field: region of electric, gravitational, magnetic or other influence.

Frequency: how often an energy wave repeats in a measure of time. Measured in Hertz (Hz) or Cycles per Second (CPS).

Geomancy: the art of designing and placing structures in the landscape so that they are in harmony with earth energies.

Geopathic Stress: non-beneficial earth energies.

Geoprosperous Energy: beneficial energies that support health

Guardians of the land: energy beings that remain in relationship to the land. Stewards.

Higher Self: an unconscious, subconscious, or super-conscious version of oneself.

Map dowsing: using a map to remotely gather information about a target.

Multiverse: a concept in quantum physics that postulates the existence of consciousness in other dimensions.

Nature Spirit: an intelligence of nature. The engineers of form.

Negative: (-) refers to the electrical charge of an object. (Does NOT mean nonbeneficial energy.)

Polarity: electrical charge of a body. Positive (+) or negative (-).

Positive: (+) electrical charge of an object. (Does NOT refer to beneficial energy.)

Psychic attack: energy directed at an individual designed to disrupt their well being.

Quantum Entanglement: "peculiar non-classical correlations that are possible between separated quantum systems."

Quantum Field: the dimensions that hold all information.

Radionics: remote detection and transformation of energy.

Radiation: the energy transfer of electromagnetic waves.

Reality: "standard reality" is defined by group consciousness. Other realities may exist at other levels of consciousness.

Remedy: something that fixes a problem.

Remote Sensing: detection at a distance.

Resonance: responding to vibrations of a particular frequency, especially by itself vibrating.

Self: The part of our consciousness that is aware of itself.

Spirit of Place / Genius Loci / Deva / Nature Spirit: various names for the spirit or natural intelligence of a place.

Spirit Team: the beneficial Beings willing and able to assist in manifesting intentions.

Subconscious Mind: part of the mind that is not fully conscious but able to influence actions.

Superconscious Mind: the (universal) mind that transcends the human conscious and subconscious minds.

Thought Form: an energy pattern produced by thoughts or emotions that can remain as an imprint at the location.

Witness: a sample of an object being sought by dowsing.

About the Author

Susan Collins is an internationally acclaimed, author, consultant and workshop leader with a dynamic, professional practice. She uses traditional dowsing tools as well as the power of heart and thought to detect and transform non-beneficial Earth, Environmental, Psychic and Other energy patterns. She has led workshops and presented at conferences across North America, the UK, in Italy, Japan and in the Middle East and was featured in "The Resonance" documentary. Susan is a Past President and Dowser of the Year of the Canadian Society of Dowsers. She is an ordained Metaphysical Minister.

Susan Collins
Personal Management Consultant
Professional Dowser
The Canadian Society of Dowsers
    Past President and Dowser of the Year,

Presenter at National Conferences
Alien Cosmic Expo: Brantford, Toronto, ON, Canada
American Society of Dowsers Conference: Lyndonville,
    Vermont; Saratoga Springs, NY, USA
ASD West Coast Convention: Santa Cruz, California, USA
ASD Southwest Conference: Flagstaff, Arizona, USA
Binnaji General Trading Co: Kuwait City, Kuwait
British Society of Dowsers Conference: Cirencester and
    Leicester, UK
Canadian Society of Dowsers Conference: Toronto, London,
    Markham, Peterborough, ON, Canada
CanAm 1, ASD/CSQ: Harrison Hot Springs, BC Canada
Questers Conferences:100 Mile House, Salmon Arm,
    Harrison Hot Springs, BC; and Olds, Alta Canada
Foundation of Mind Being Research: Palo Alto, CA, USA
International Dowsers: Sterling, Scotland
Italian Dowsing Society: Bologna, Italy
Japanese Society of Dowsers: Kakegawa, Tokyo, Japan
Ozark Research Institute Conference: Fayetteville, AR, USA

Many regional meetings and events across America.

Workshop Rentals
Susan's curriculum is available on Vimeo.
https://vimeo.com/susancollinsdowser/vod_pages

Publications
Anemone Magazine, Japan
What's New in Dowsing, CSD journal, Canada
The Quester, CSQ/CSD quarterly journal, Canada
The American Dowser, ASD Quarterly Digest, USA

Dowsing Today, British Society of Dowsers, U.K.
Journal, The Dowsing Society of NSW, Australia,
Revista Cientifica Radiestesia, Dowsing Society of
  Chile
Human Spirit Magazine, Ontario, Canada
Vitality Magazine, KI Awareness – Ontario, Canada

Film and Television
Resonance Film
https://vimeo.com/ondemand/theresonance
City TV; Rogers TV; VRLand News.

YouTube Channel
www.youtube.com/c/susancollinsdowser

Susan Collins Print and Kindle Books

Check Susan's Kindle and Amazon Print on Demand
books in the "**Complete Guide to Dowsing**" series.

Print books by Susan Collins:
    Bridge Matter and Spirit with Dowsing
    Get Healthy with Dowsing
    Get Happy with Dowsing
    Dowse for Feng Shui and Space Clearing
    Meet Alien Energy with Dowsing
    Meet Orbs with Dowsing
    Water Wells: What a Dowser Needs to Know
    Life Cards Oracle System

To order books and tools, or to arrange a workshop or
personal session, contact Susan at
susan@dowser.ca   www.dowser.ca

Bridge Matter and
Spirit with Dowsing

Get Healthy with
Dowsing

Dowsing for
Feng Shui and Space
Clearing

Meet Alien Energy
with Dowsing

Dowsing That Works

Dowsing Triage
Find and Fix Energy
Problems

Meet Orbs with
Dowsing

Water Wells: What
a Dowser Needs to
Know

Life Cards
Oracle Set

Dowsing That Works
Japanese Edition

*I wish you happiness as
your journey unfolds.*
Susan